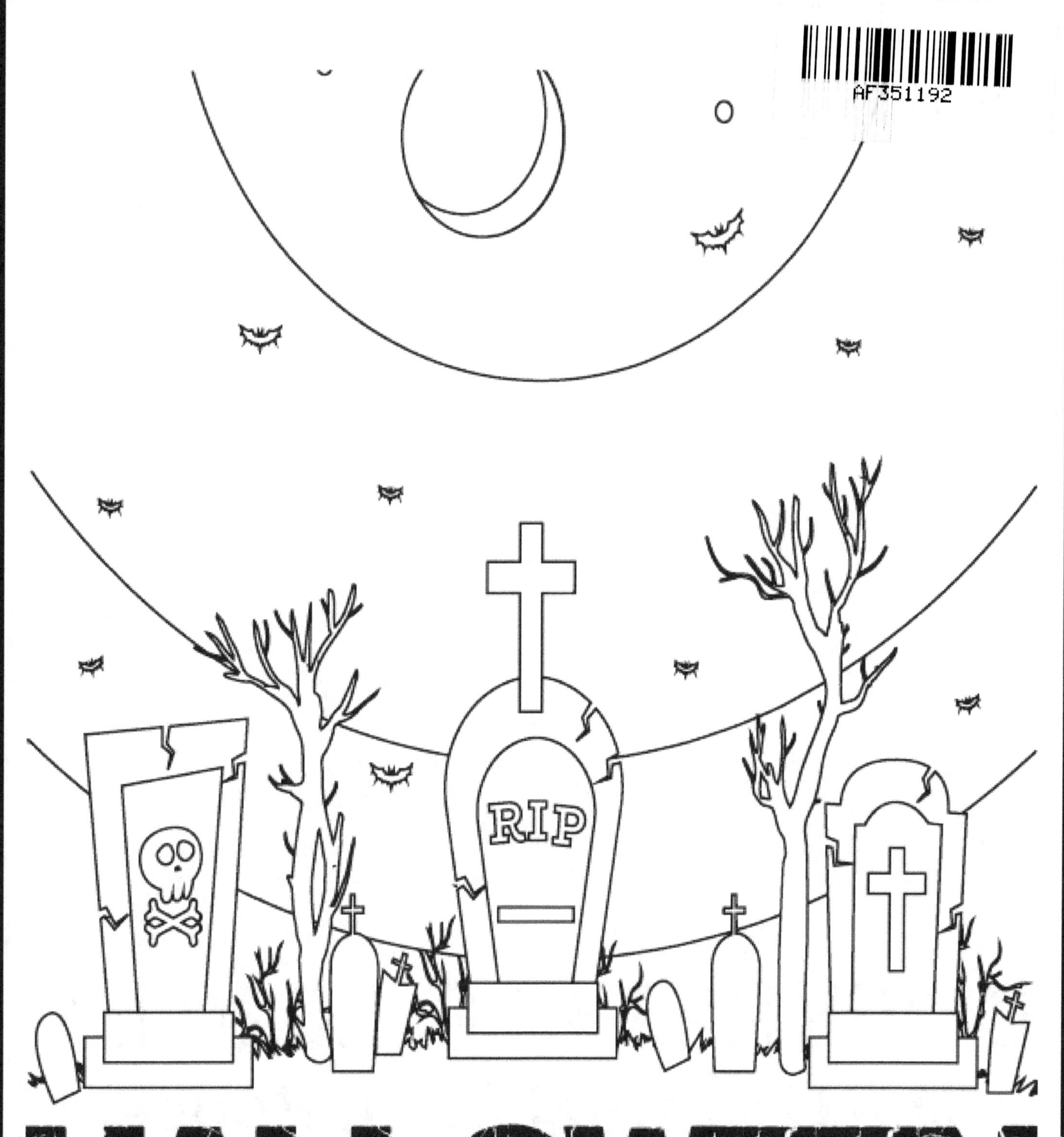

HALLOWEEN
COLORING BOOK FOR TEENS

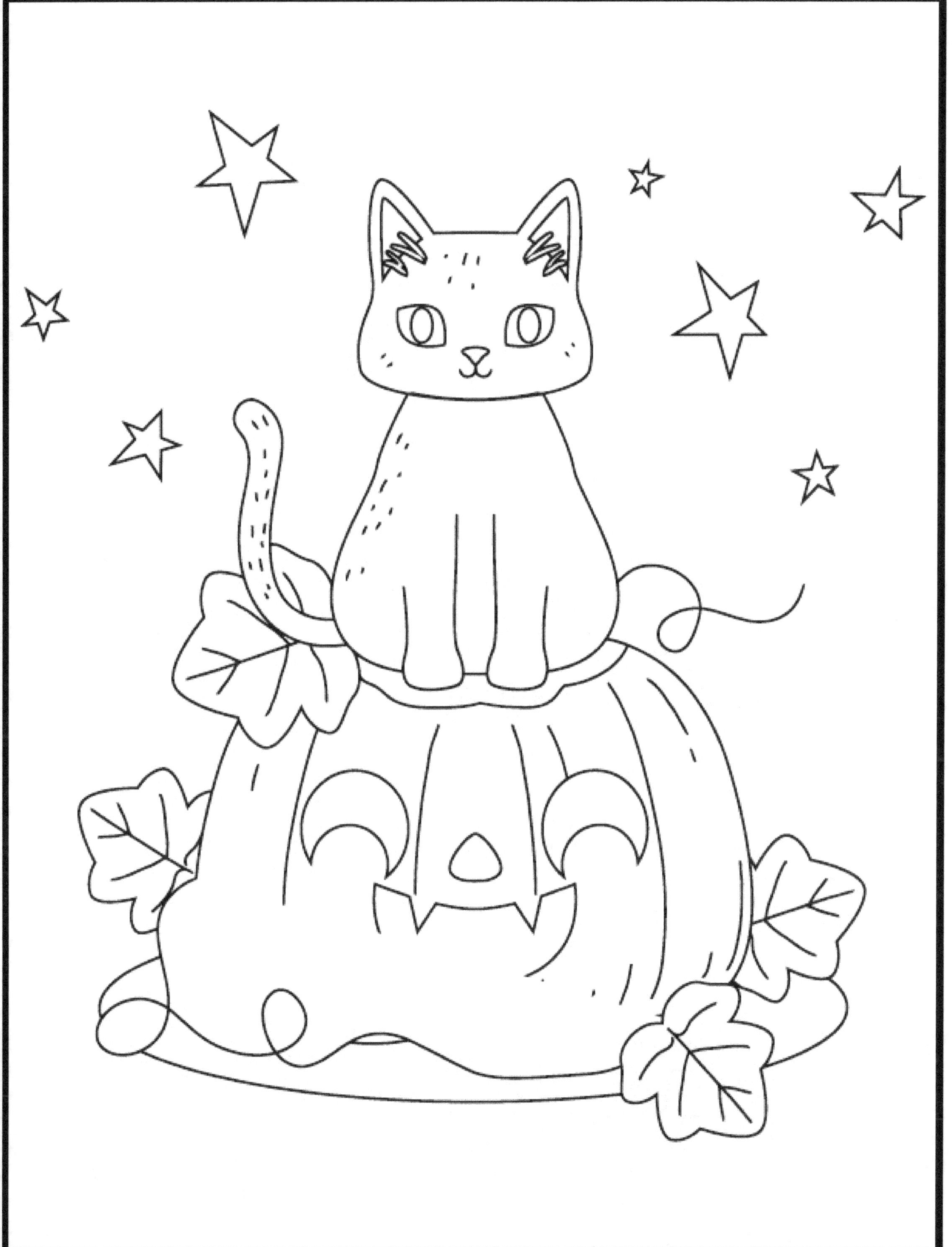

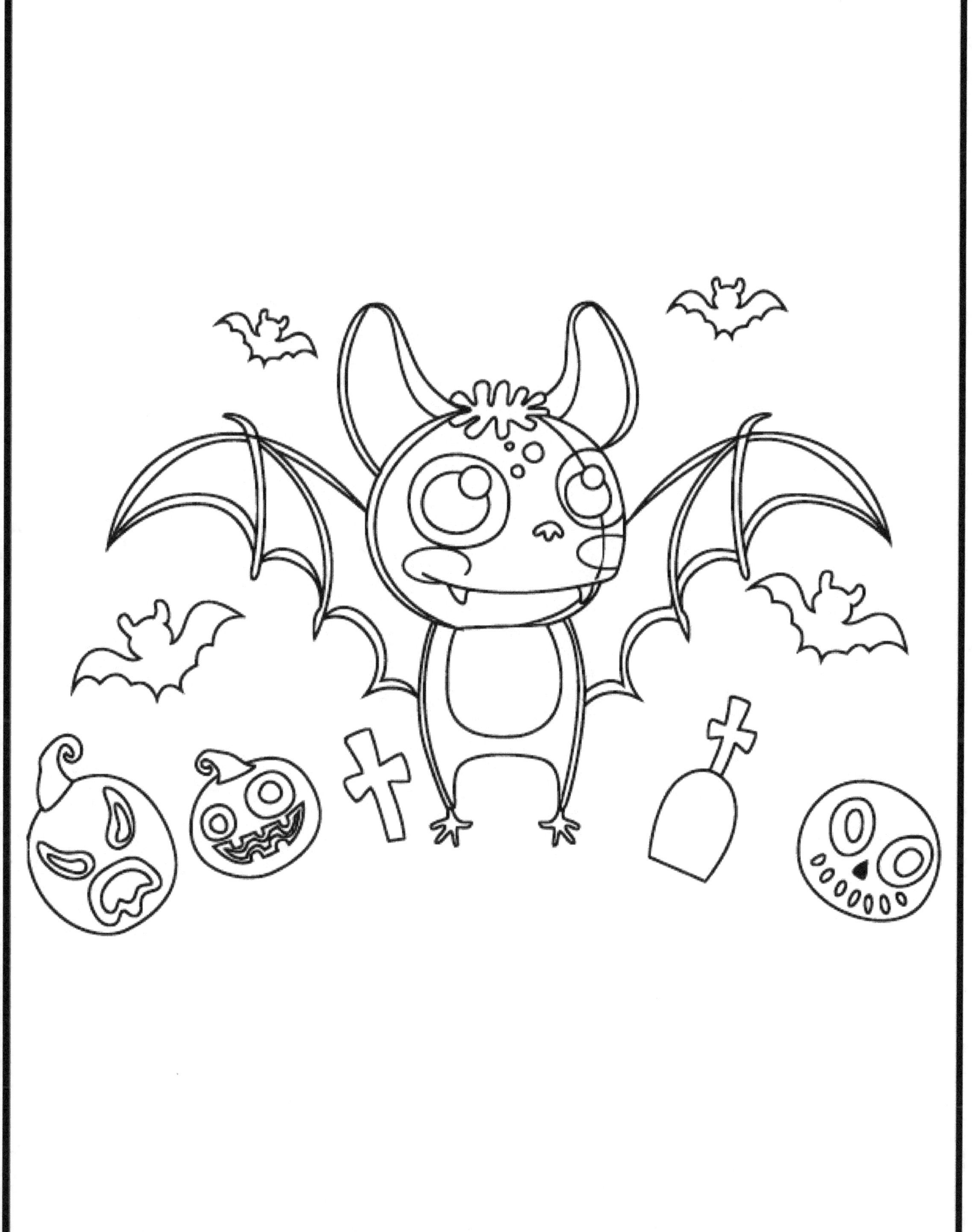

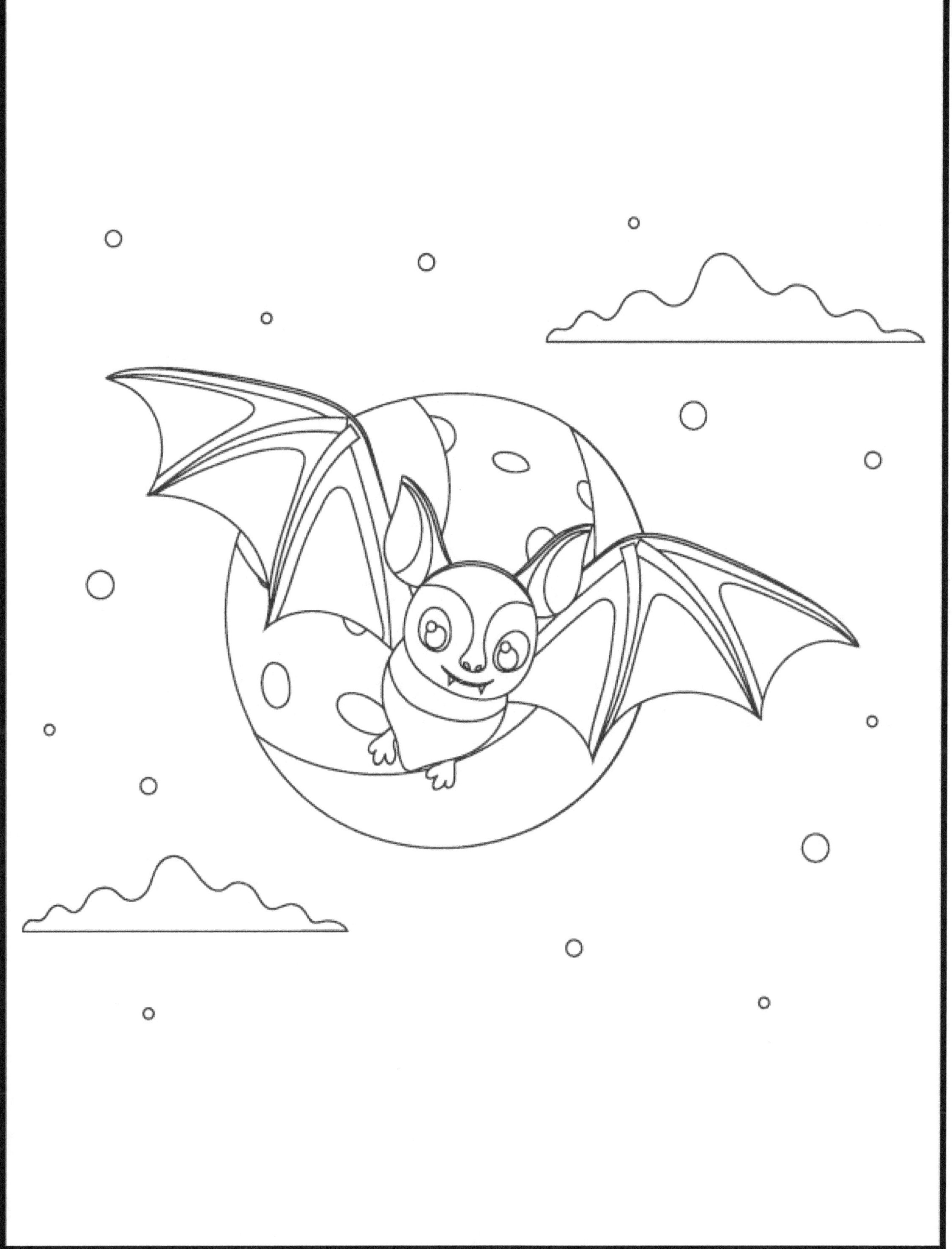

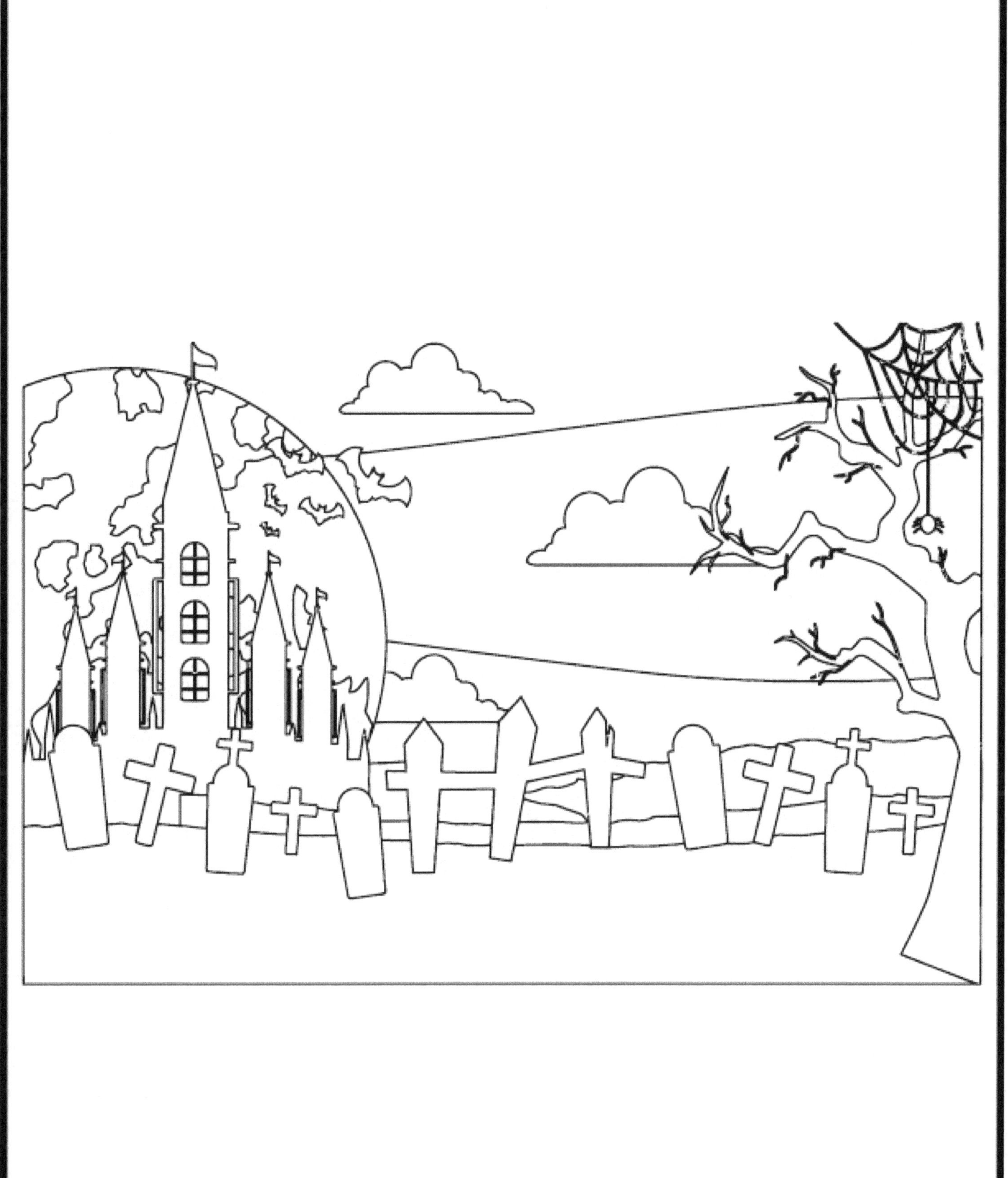

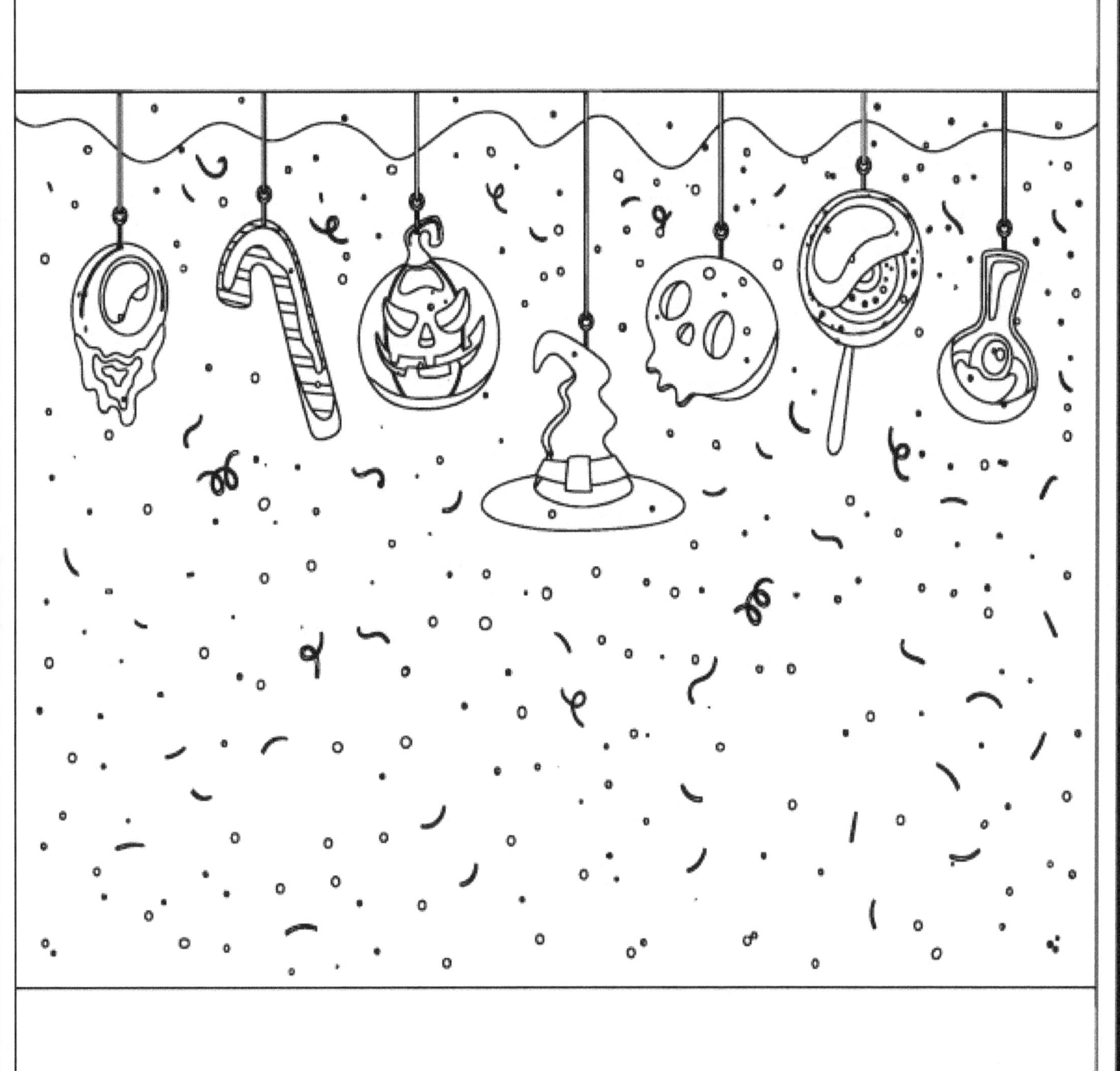

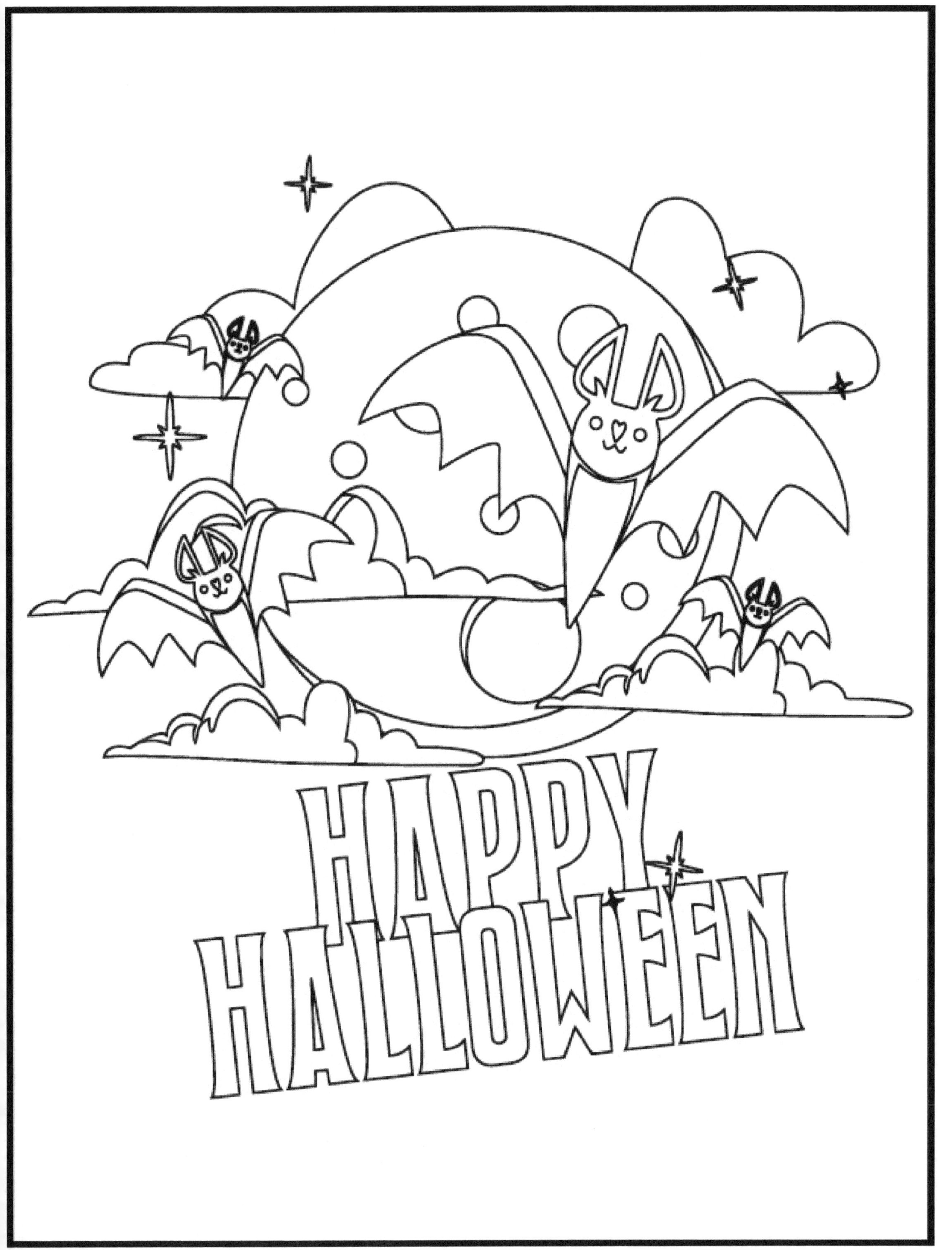

HAPPY HALLOWEEN

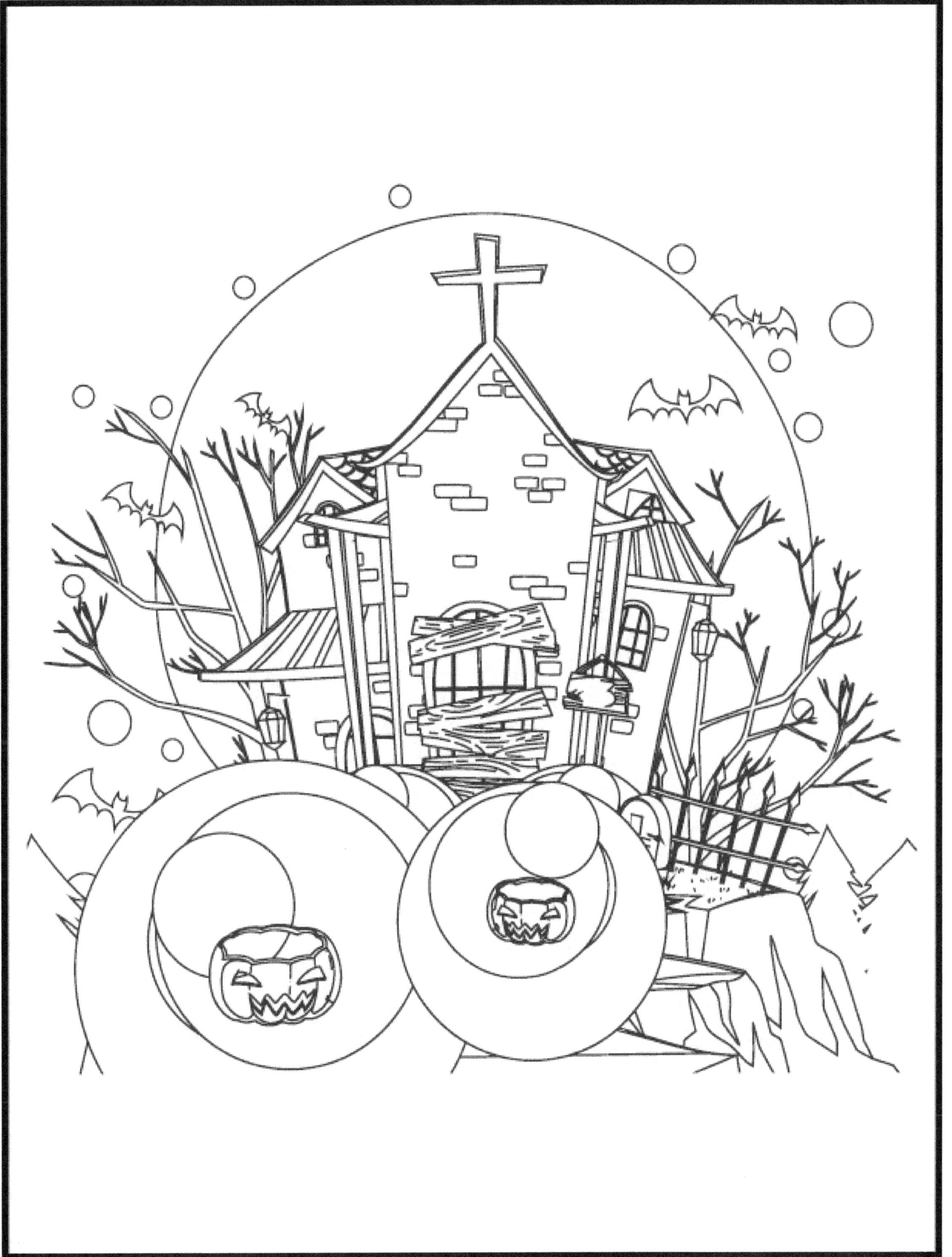

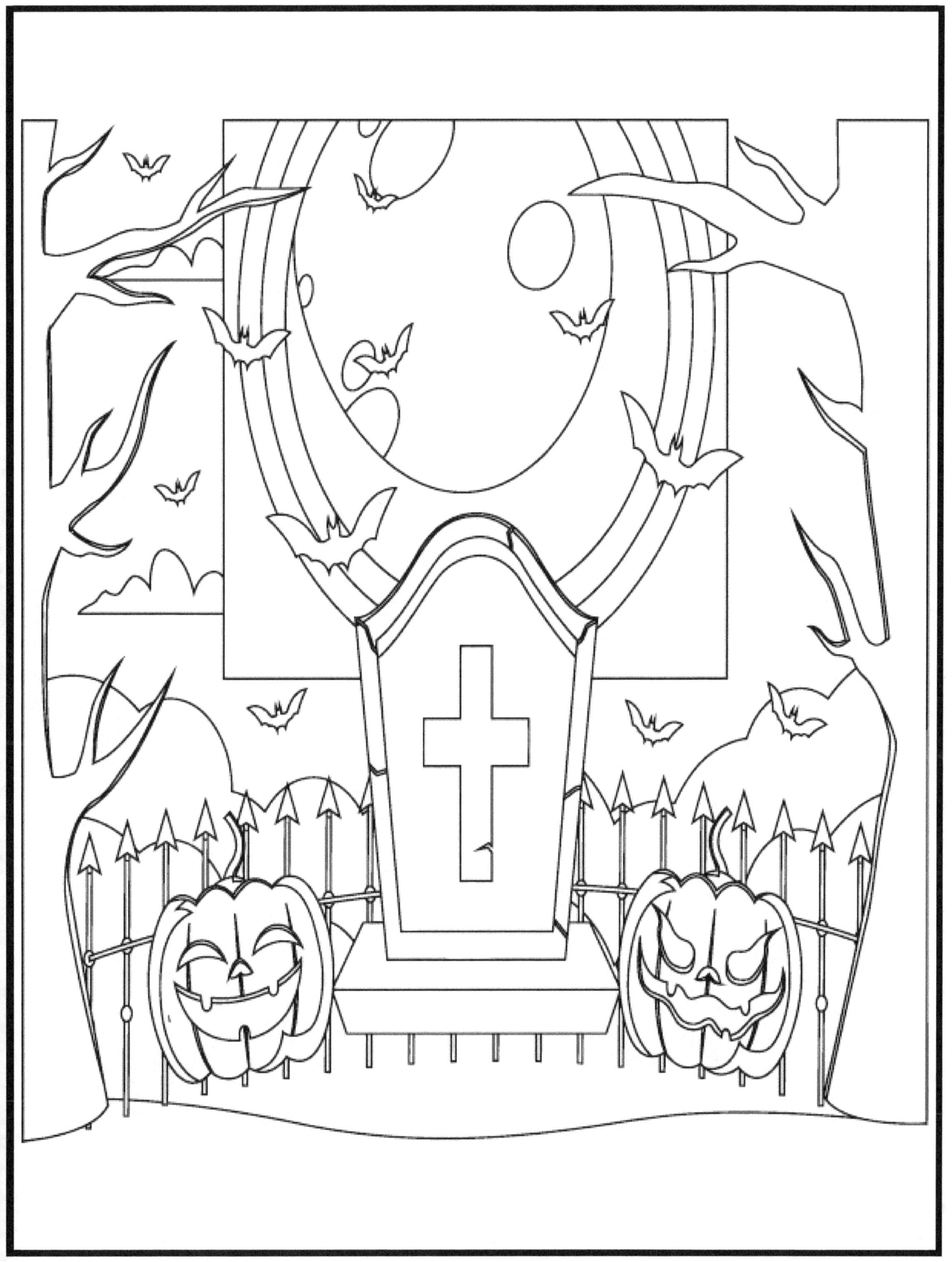

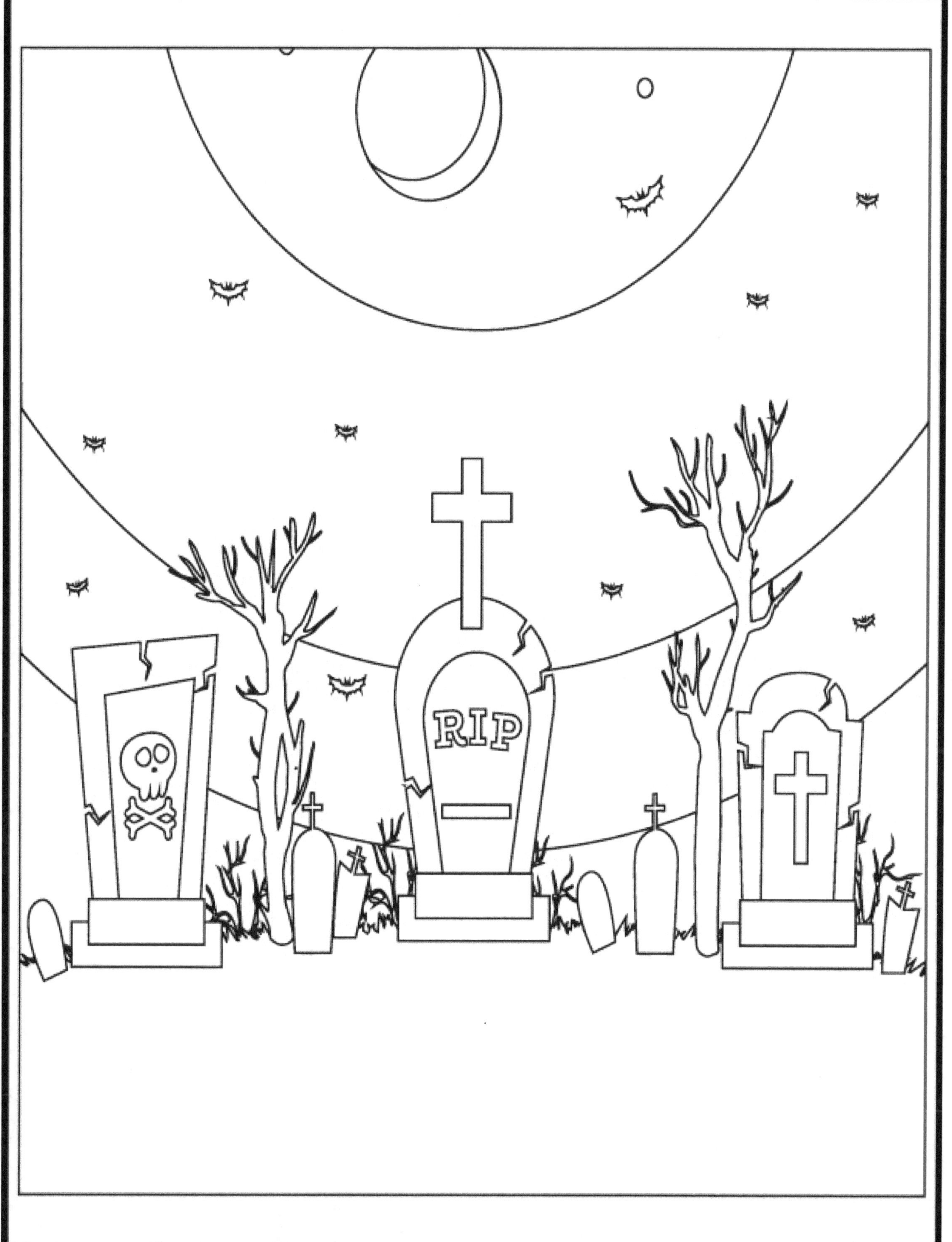

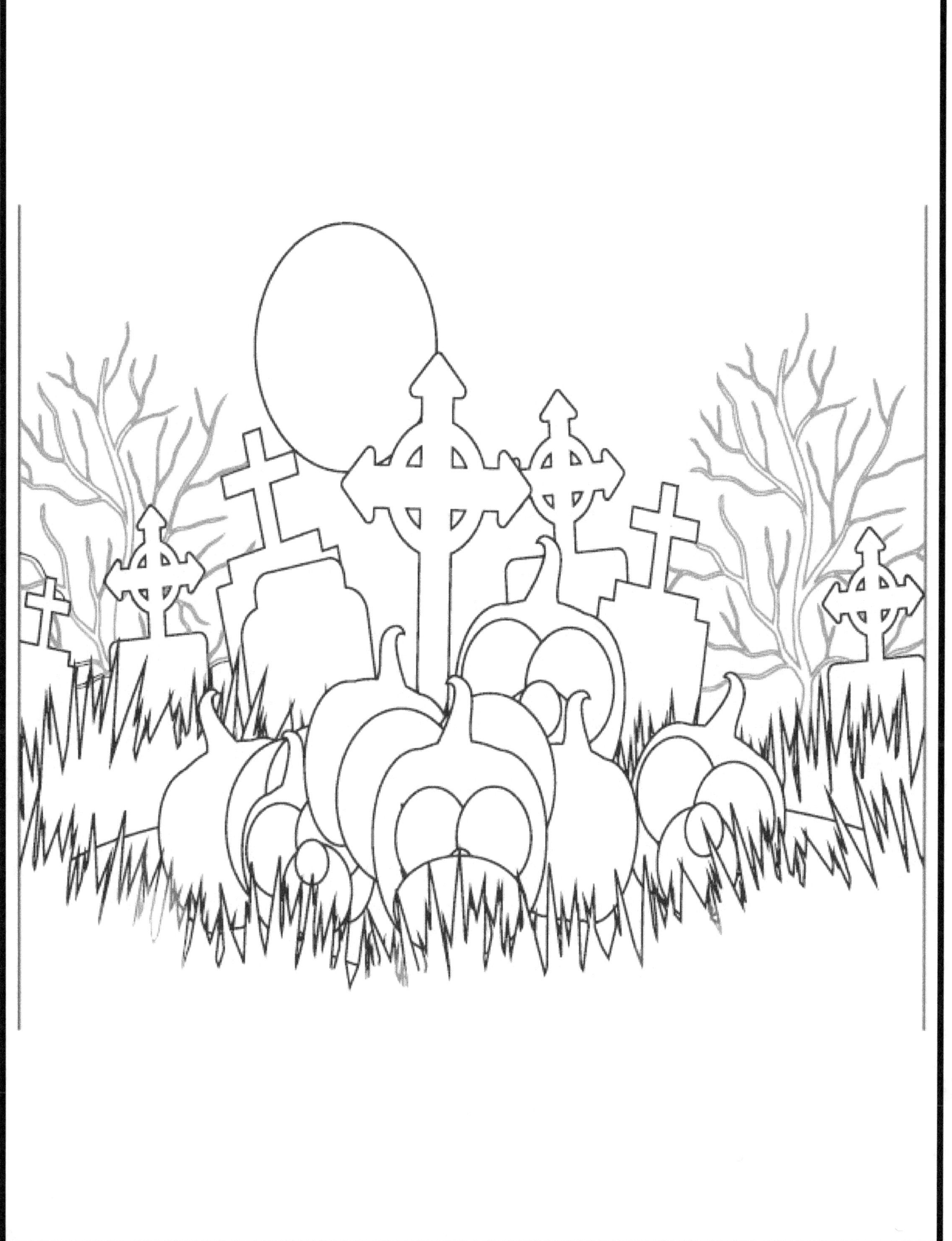

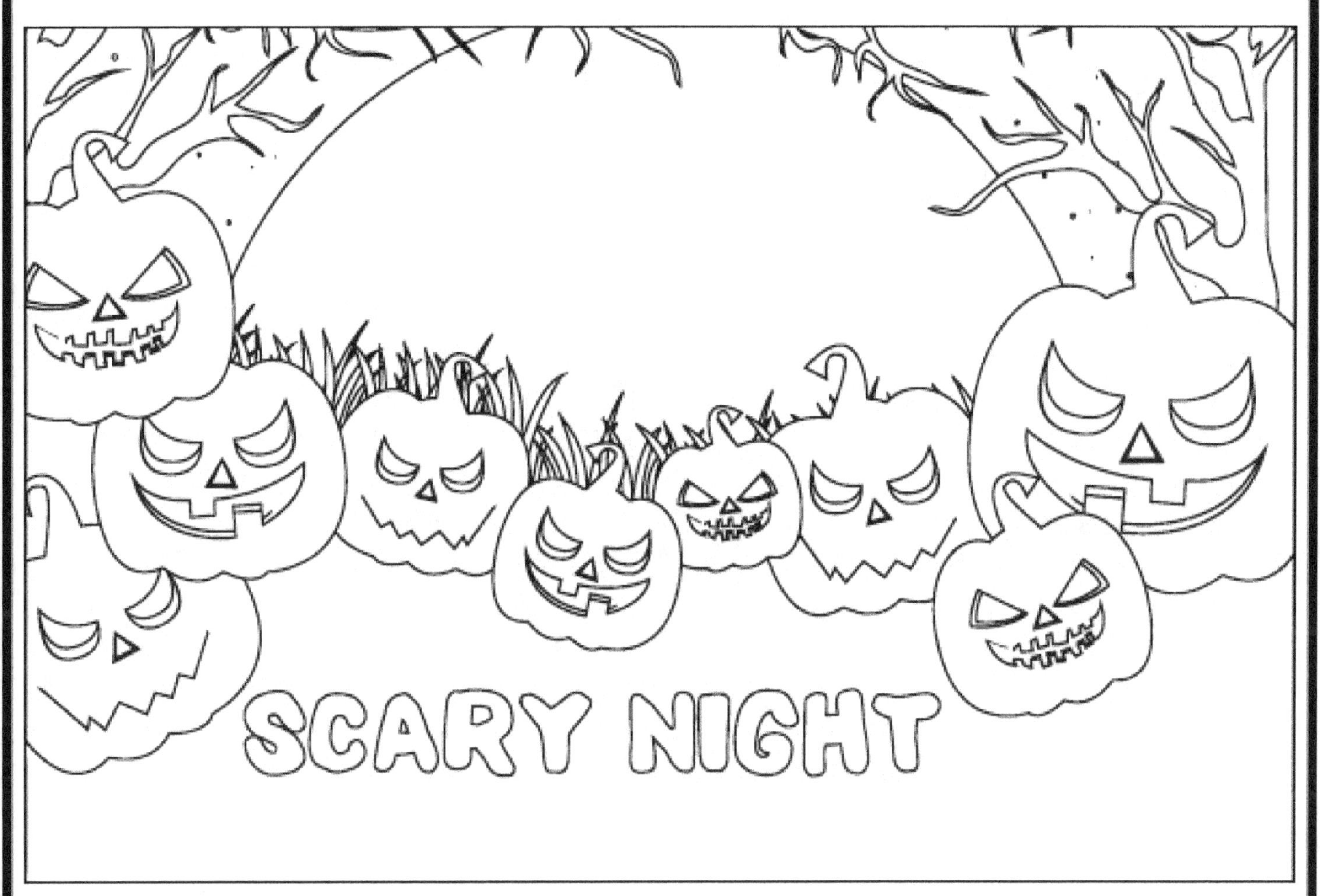

SCARY NIGHT

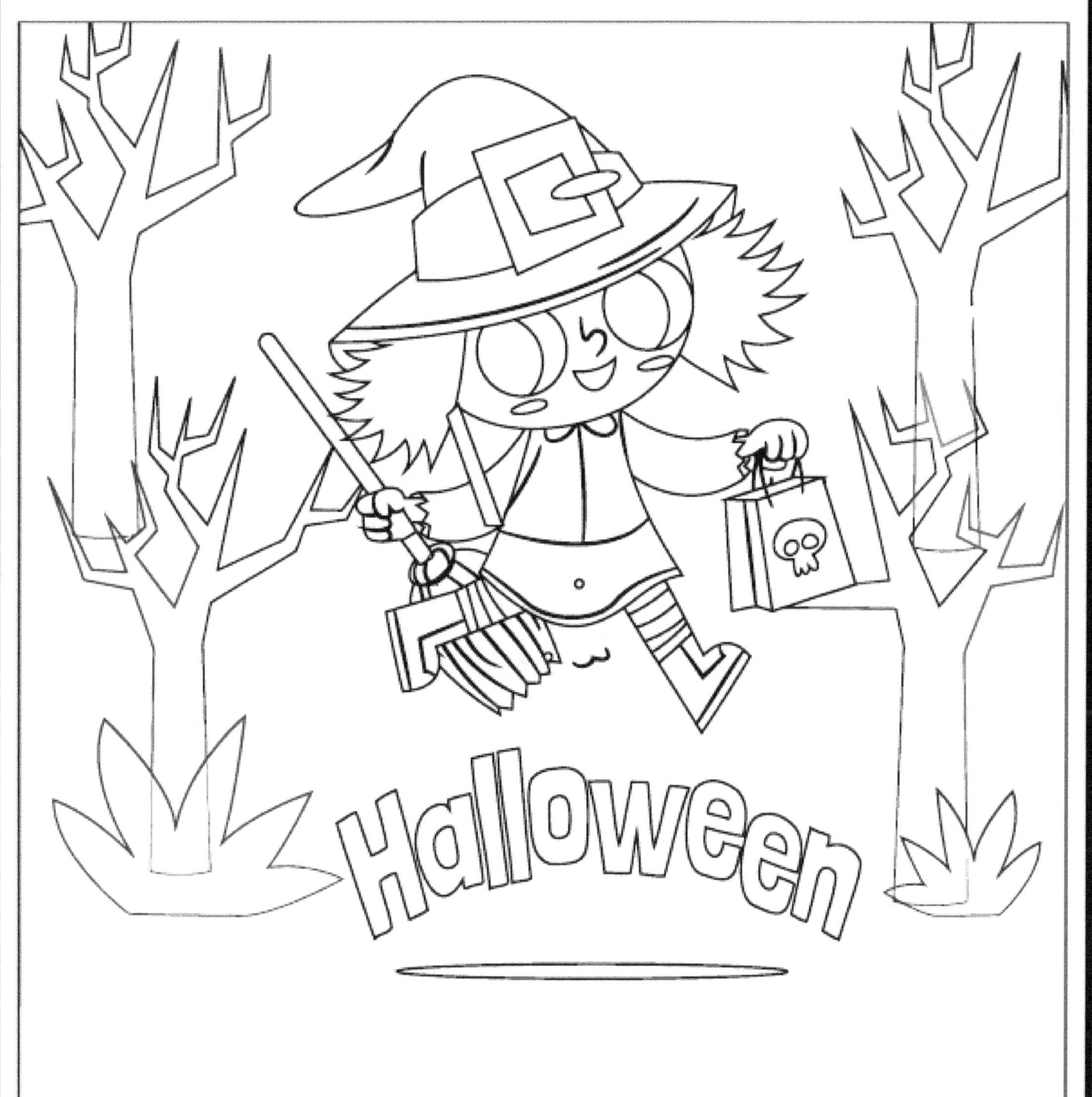
Halloween

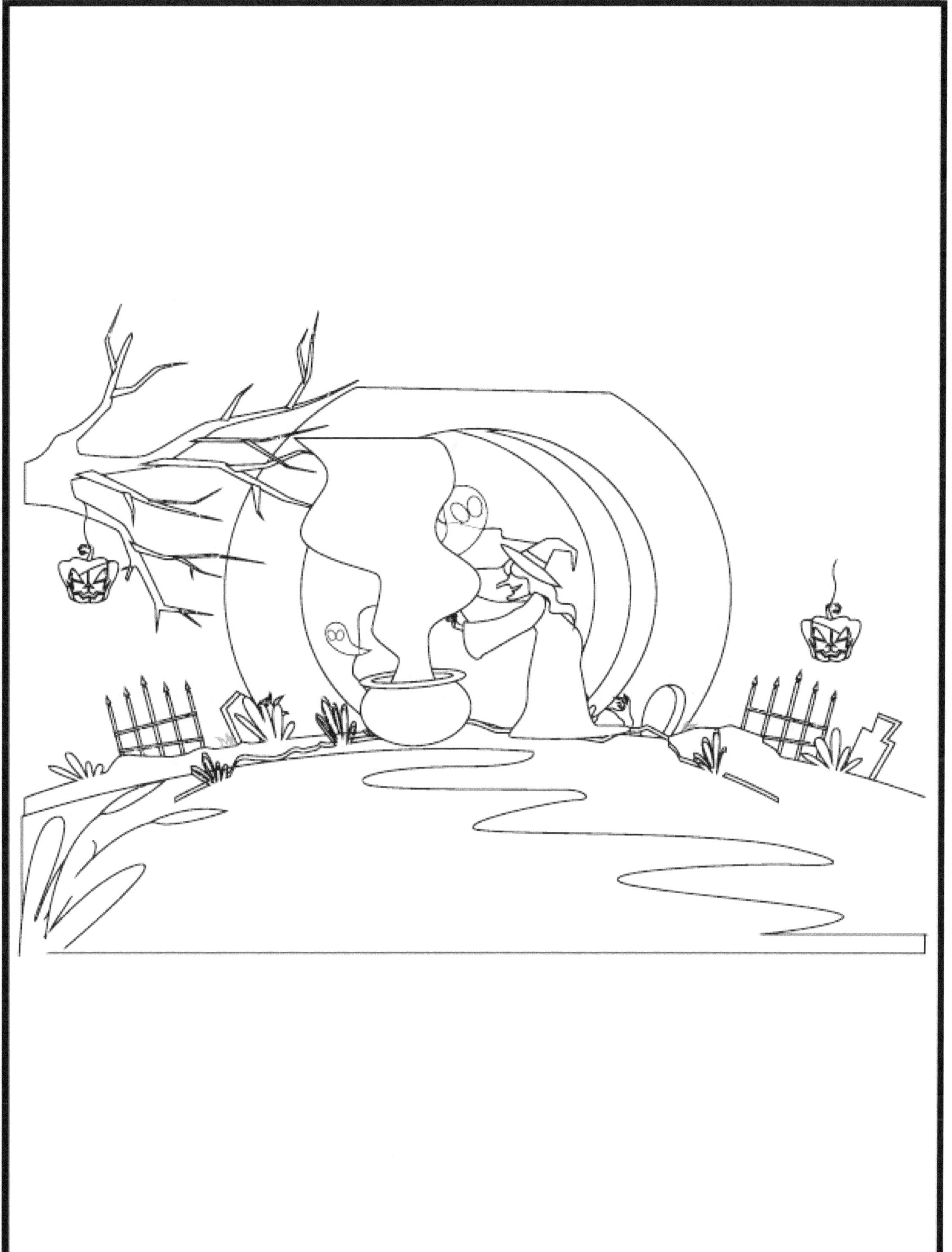

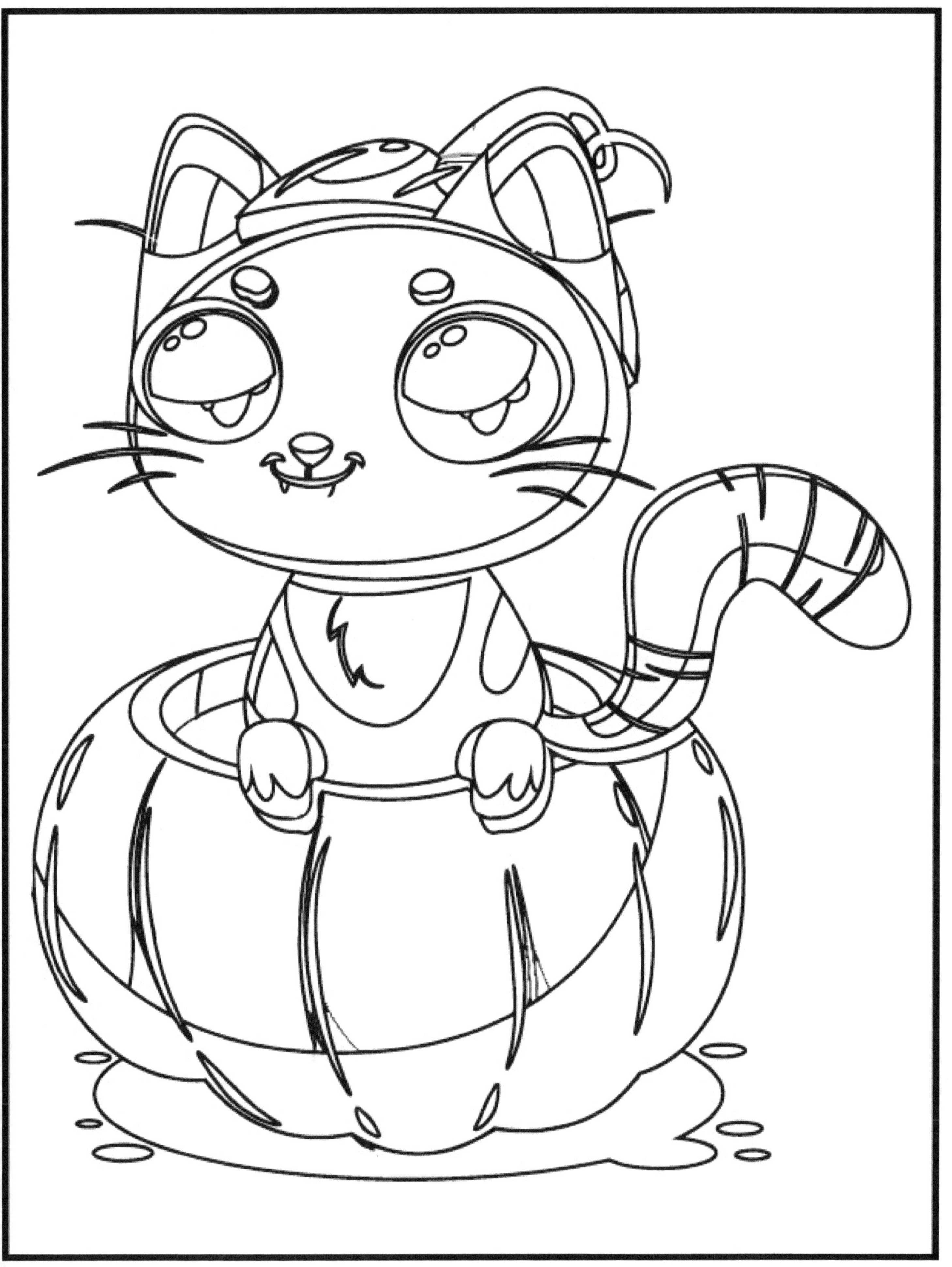

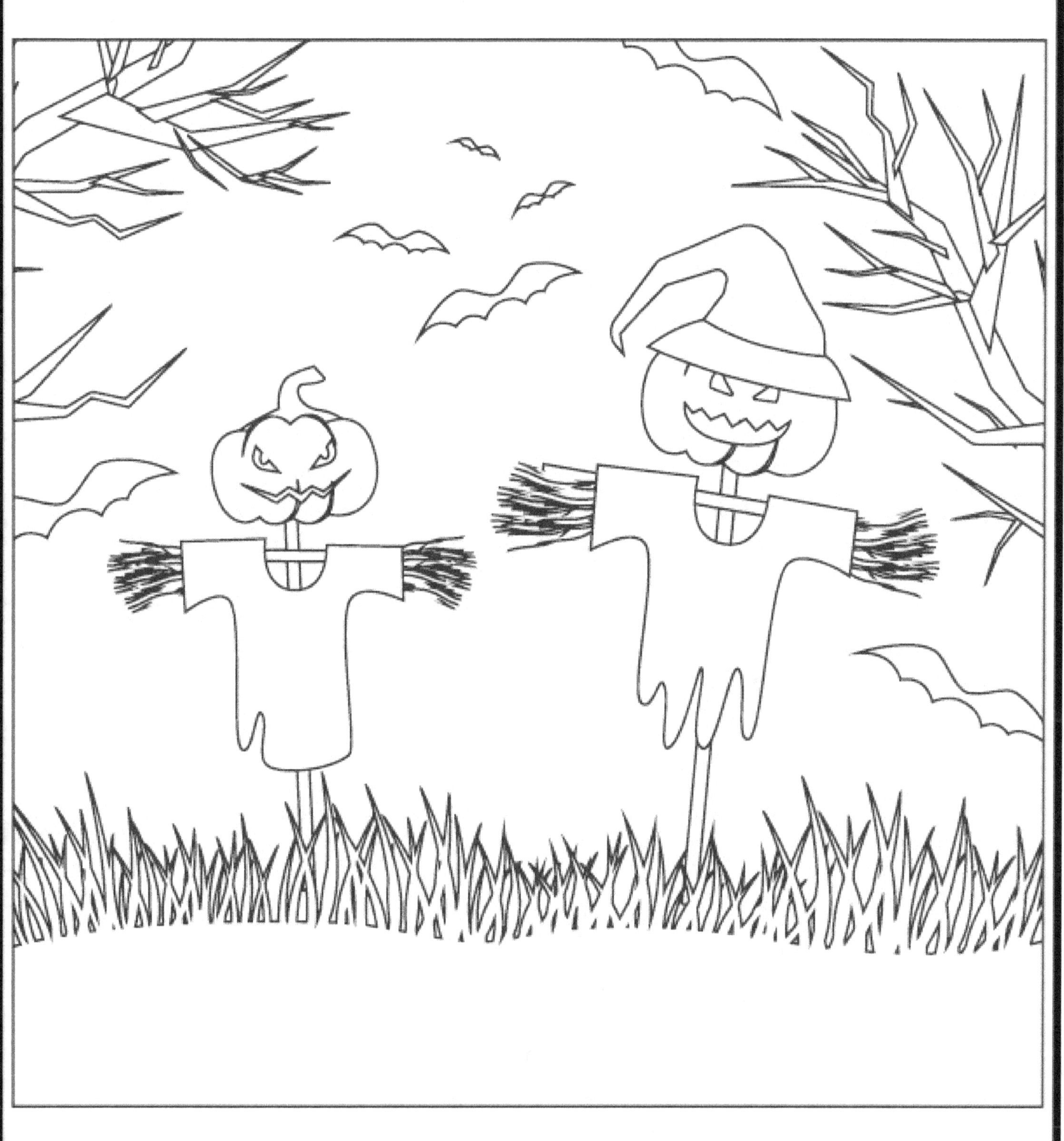

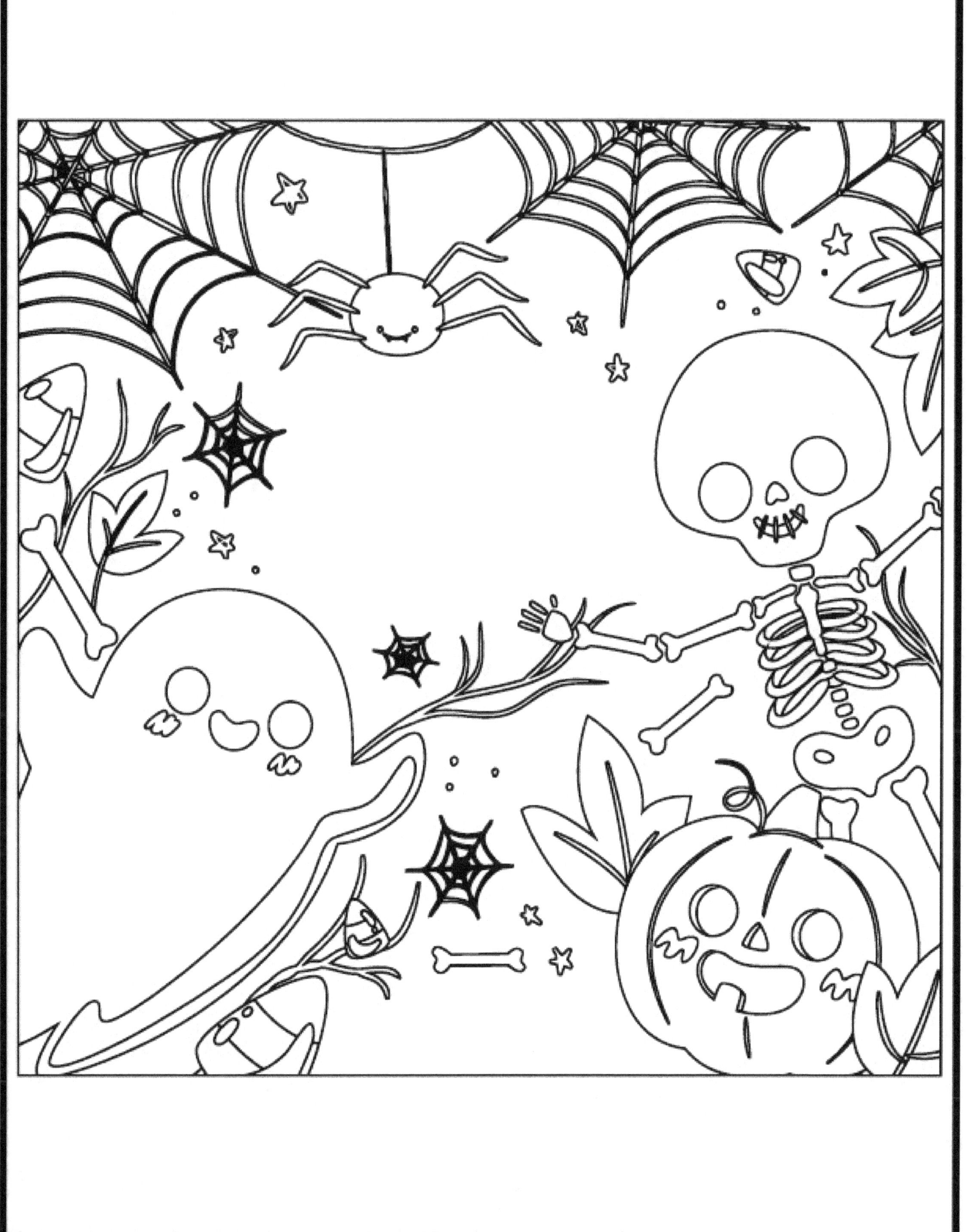

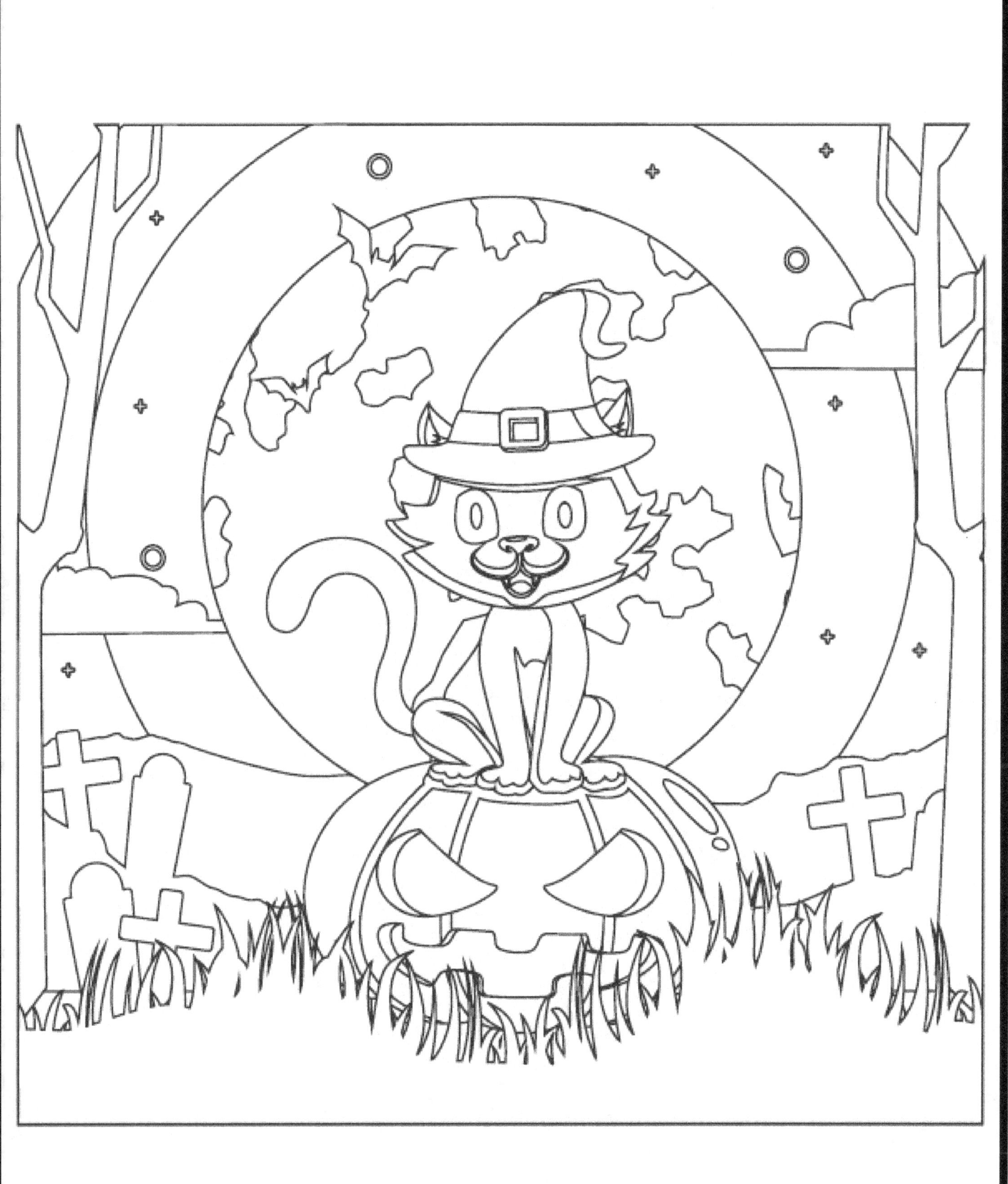

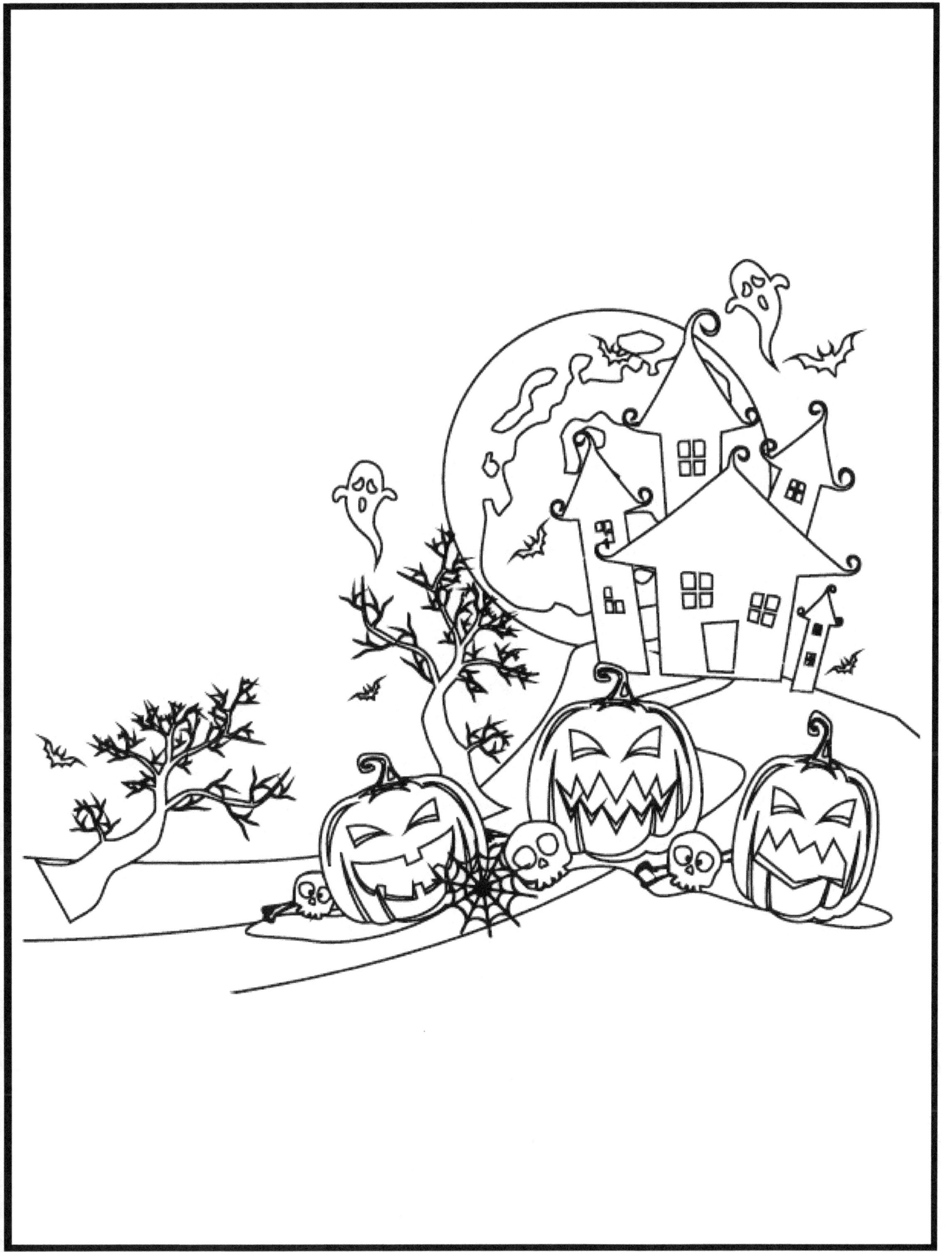

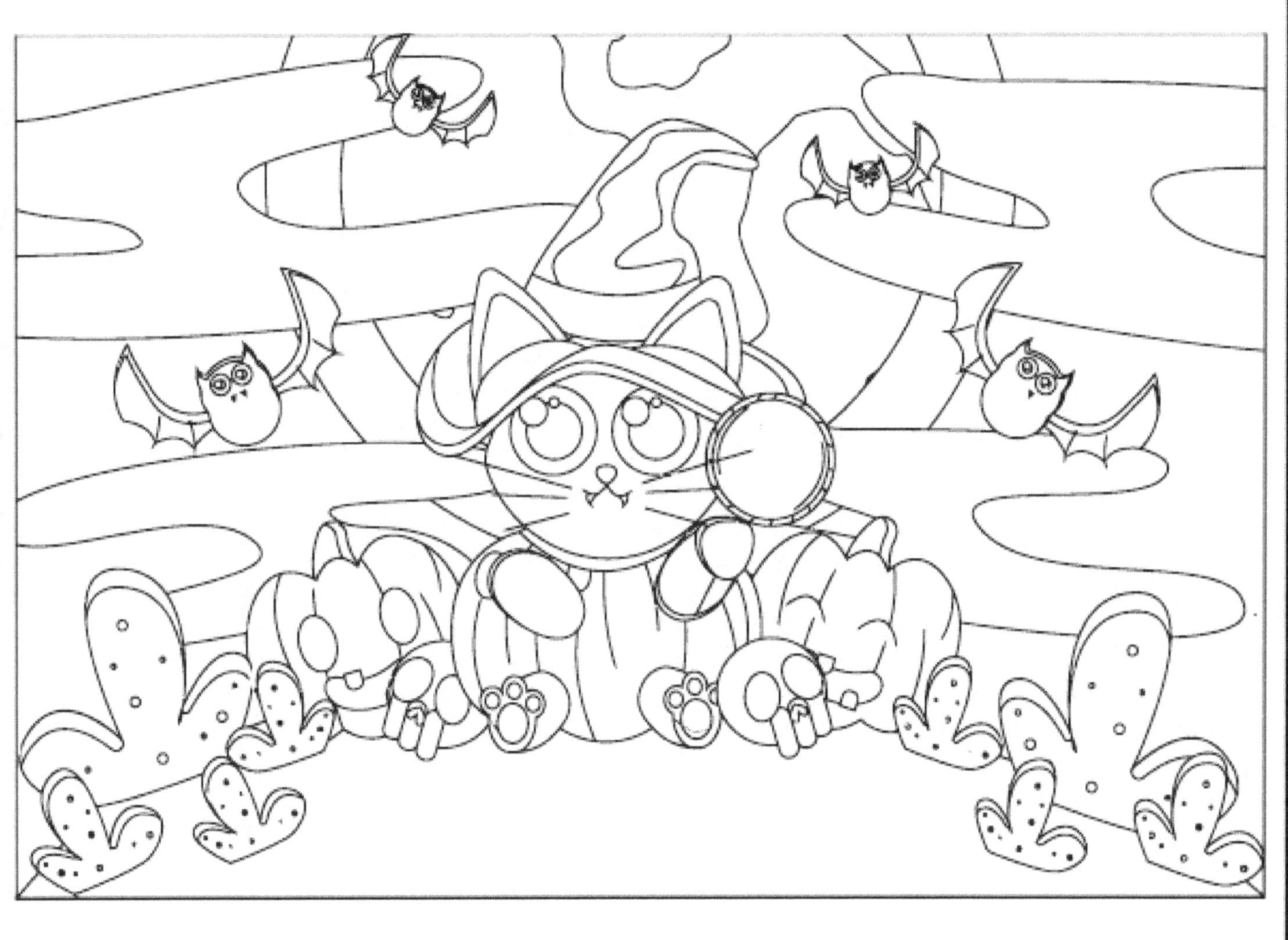

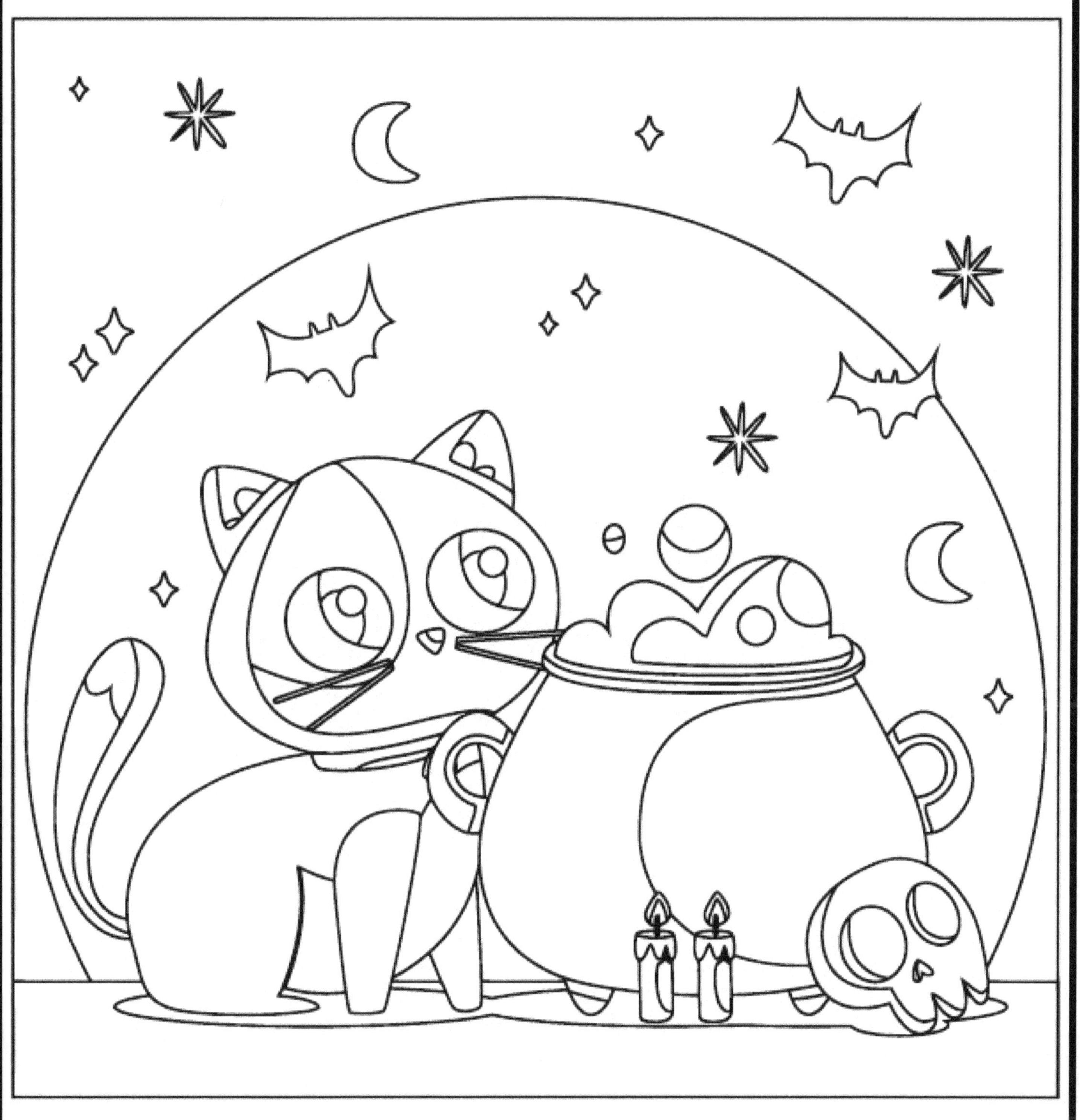

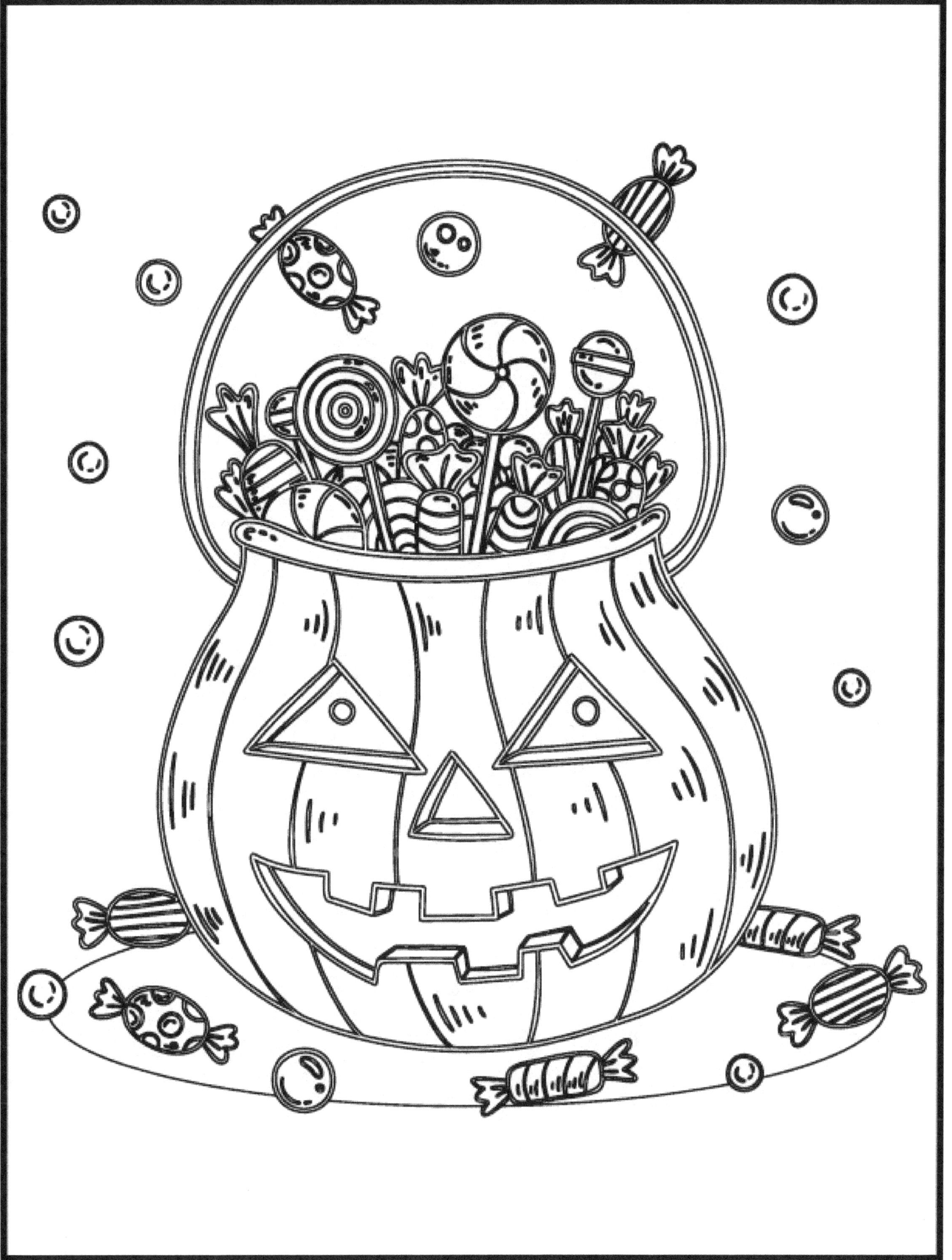

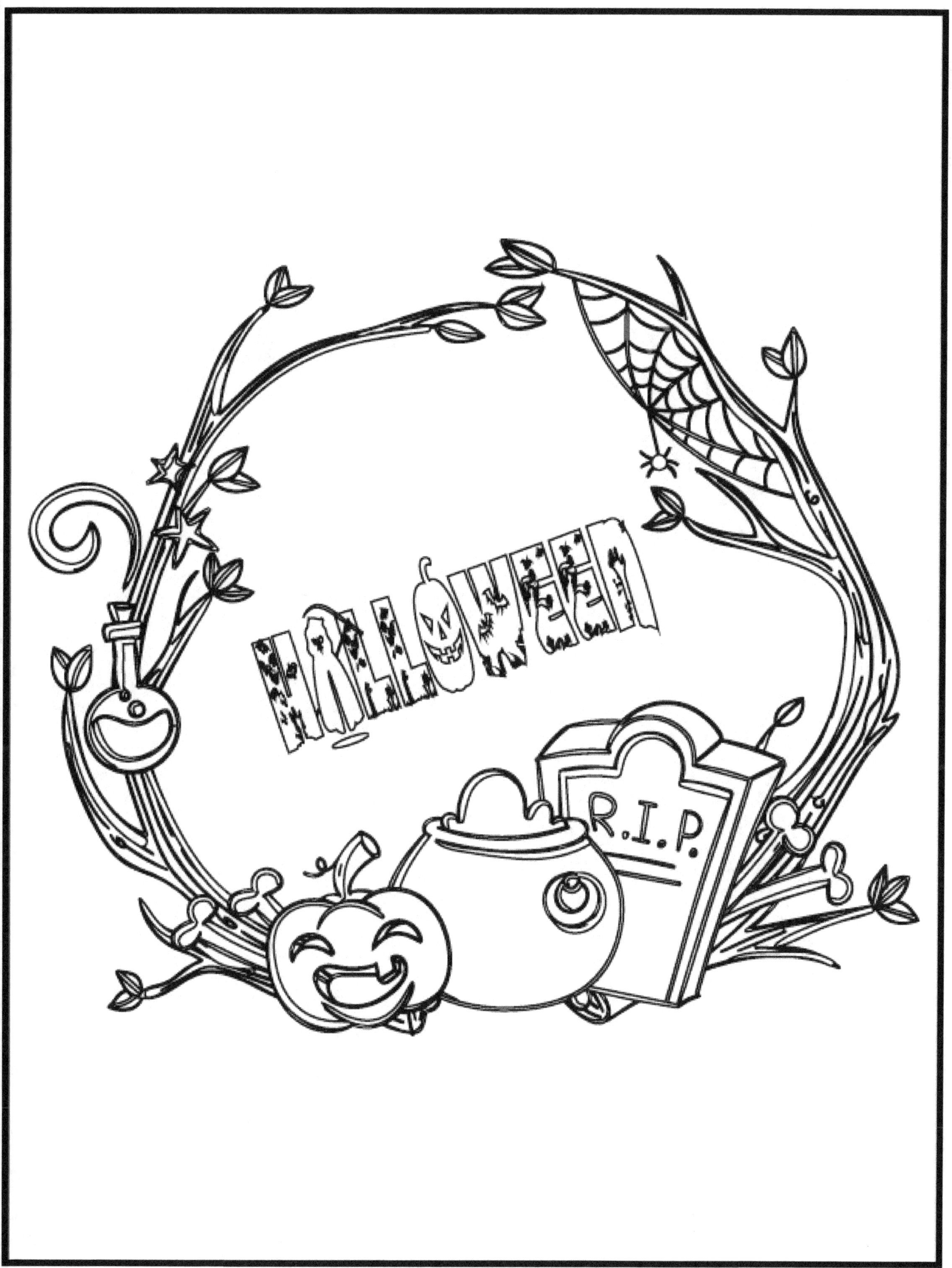

HALLOWEEN
R.I.P.

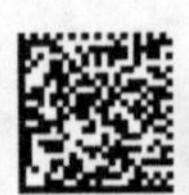